D1799506

Richard Austin's

More
WESTCOUNTRY
ANIMAL
MAGIC

HALSGROVE

First published in Great Britain in 2003

Copyright © 2003 Richard Austin

*All rights reserved. No part of this publication may be reproduced,
stored in a retrieval system, or transmitted in any form or by any
means without the prior permission of the copyright holder.*

British Library Cataloguing-in-Publication Data
A CIP record for this title is available from the British Library

ISBN 1 84114 291 3

HALSGROVE

Halsgrove House
Lower Moor Way
Tiverton, Devon EX16 6SS
Tel: 01884 243242
Fax: 01884 243325
email: sales@halsgrove.com
website: www.halsgrove.com

Printed by D'Auria Industrie Grafiche Spa, Italy

FOREWORD

It was the first night of the *Western Morning News* conversion from a
broadsheet to a quality tabloid newspaper – and it was chaos!

As one new-shaped page after another went through our system there
were few which did not need urgent remedial action.

On the new-look weather and Westcountry View spread a hole had appeared through
miscalculation. 'Fill it with a picture – any picture', I bawled. We were over deadline.

The Picture Editor produced a lovely shot of a couple of monkeys.
'Make a feature of it', I barked. 'Call it Animal Magic'.

A few short weeks later Animal Magic was among our readers' favourite features.
Later we moved it to give it more prominence in its own slot because it was so popular.

Richard Austin, the most gifted newspaper photographer I have ever
worked with, is Animal Magic's most consistent contributor.

This is the second volume of Richard's Animal Magic pictures – produced
in response to demand after the first was a huge success.

They're just as fresh and compelling – every bit as much enjoyable. A genuine collectors' item.

Barrie Williams
Editor
Western Morning News

Feathers ruffle on a female Peregrine falcon,
perched on a church tower in Exeter.

INTRODUCTION

Welcome to the second *Animal Magic* book and to even more pictures
of our animal friends from the region, both wild and tame.
Being a newspaper photographer in a world of fast-moving news stories,
and the need to be somewhere else at the drop of a hat is frantic enough,
but it is always a refreshing moment when I get the chance to
slow down and take time out for an animal story.
Living in a region with such an abundance of wildlife and animal
welfare organisations there is no shortage of photo-opportunities
for a committed animal photographer.

As with the first *Animal Magic,* this book celebrates the many species
of birds and animals found throughout the region, and the people
who care passionately for them.

Richard Austin
2003

ACKNOWLEDGEMENTS

My sincere thanks go to the businesses, individuals and organisations listed below
whose help and co-operation over the years has been invaluable.

Barrie Williams (*Editor Western Morning News*); Michael Cranmer (Picture Editor *Western Morning News*);
Secret World Wildlife Rescue; Barbara Austin; Karen Andriunas & Saker Falconry; RSPB; Paignton Zoo;
Trevor Beer; Chris Murray at Pennywell Farm and Wildlife Centre; Buckfast Butterflies & Dartmoor Otter
Sanctuary; Dartmoor Wildlife Park; Chris Burnett, RSPCA; Pauline Kidner; Ellie West; Nikki Hawkins;
Ray Brind; Abbotsbury Swannery; Katrina Lindfield; Dartmoor Miniature Pony & Animal Centre;
Devon & Cornwall Police; David Disney; The Donkey Sanctuary; League Against Cruel Sports; Rosemary Willets;
Axhayes Cats Protection; Diane Randall, Woodlands, Bickleigh Mill; Cricket St Thomas;
Andrew Freemantle; Gilly Greed (One Voice Media); Wild Meadow Farm; Susan Thomas;
Jeanette Downing; Rex Features.

And a big thankyou to anyone whose name has been undeservedly omitted from the above.

DEDICATION

TO DIANA, MATTHEW AND MADDIE.

REMEMBERING: NORMAN AUSTIN.

A rare Little Bittern on the banks of the canal in Exeter. Birdwatchers from all over Britain had descended on the canal banks, some waiting for 5 hours for the bird to come out of the bushes. I had only been there for 2 minutes and not only did the Little Bittern appear, he also had a fish in his mouth!

Nikki Hawkins at Secret World Wildlife Rescue with a very young Roe Deer, despite all of Nikki's tender loving care, sadly the little deer died.

He could have been called a cat burglar, but the black moggy climbed out of the upstairs window and on to the top of the open downstairs window, and then down to the floor. What an athlete!

Almost round-the-clock feeding was required for this newborn giraffe at Paignton Zoo after his mother had refused to look after her little calf.

How to help a three-legged tortoise get around...?
Ask your local vet to fix him up with a tube of
superglue and a toy skateboard.

This trio of young hares (leverets) was found cuddled up to their dead mother by a caring farmer.

Three young robins waiting to be fed by the staff at Secret World Wildlife Rescue.

Residents all along the south coast are fed up with seagulls nesting on their roofs and have even resorted to placing barbed wire on the chimneys to warn them off. Theses pictures show what happened when one of the gulls got tangled in the wire: the fire brigade had to be called to release the bird who was none the worse for his experience, although the noise from the other gulls who showed up was deafening.

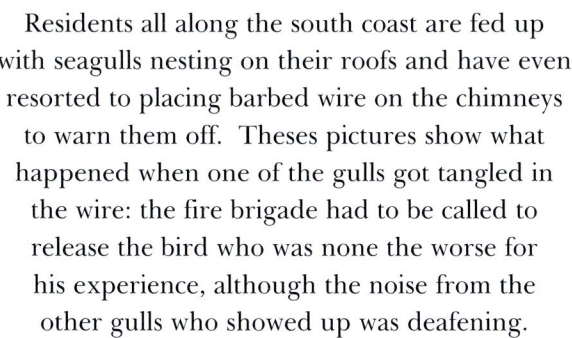

The silent but deadly flight
of a hunting Barn Owl.

This cheeky nest-making jackdaw
pulls the hair from the cow's back for
a soft and cosy lining to her nest.

The unusual story of the baby Tree Creeper who got stuck on a flypaper trap inside someone's greenhouse. Margarine was recommended to dissolve the glue still on his feathers.

A mini heat wave, and this gosling was more than happy to be cooled down with the watering can.

It was fascinating watching these House Martins gather mud for their nests from the banks of the River Otter in Tipton St John.

Katrina Lindfield teaches her young goslings to fly through the lanes of East Devon.

Two dogs, miles apart. The spaniel was recovering from an operation after swallowing two or three Elvis Presley tapes; you can imagine the newspaper headlines, 'Hound Dog', 'Old Shep' and many others. The other is the late Bracken, an old timer who loved to put his head through the gate in Barnstaple just to see who was around.

Tubes for the rats to play in, and a cuddle for a newborn gosling and goat kid.

This male lion enjoys a good early-morning yawn at the Dartmoor Wildlife Park.

Young parrots being brought up by hand, eating off a specially shaped spoon.

I came across this grasshopper eating cyclamen petals in my garden, and was attracted by the colour and the light.

Springtime is a busy period for the birds. These swallows feed their babies, and the blue-tits set about nest building.

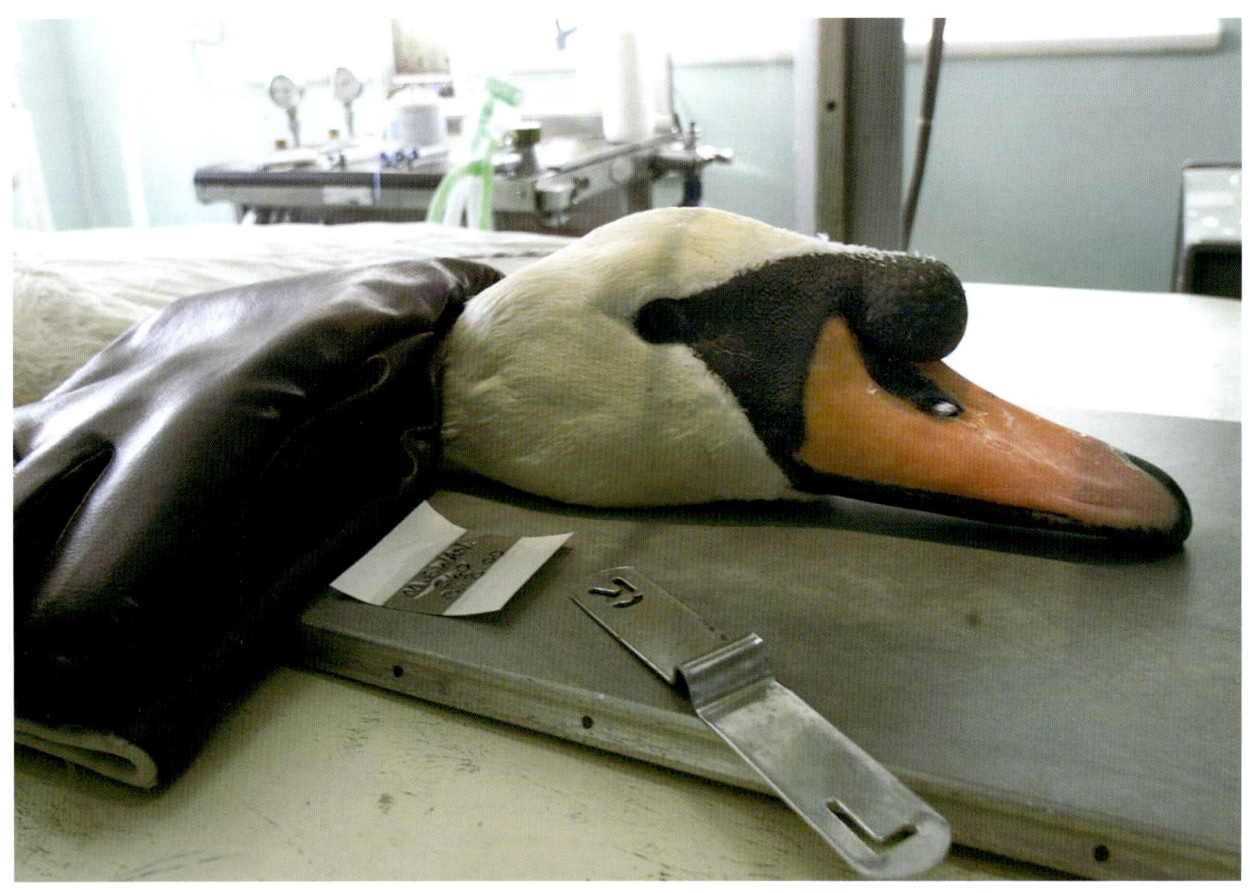

As a press photographer there are some animal stories which highlight incredible cruelty to animals and birds. This poor swan had been shot not once, but twice, in the head with an air gun and was still very much alive. The main picture shows him about to have an X-ray and in order to keep him still a bean-bag was placed on his neck, all of which he took in his stride.

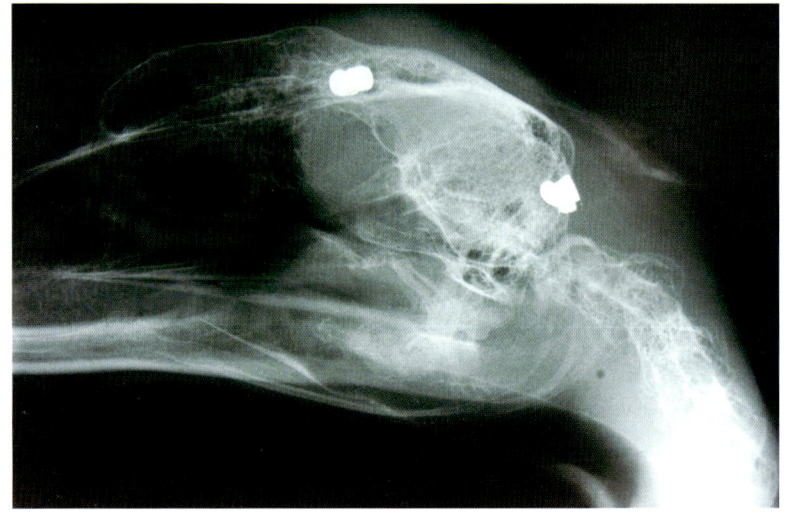

Who's taking who for a walk...? Two characters on the Grand Western Canal in Tiverton, Devon, where Ben the barge-horse and the collie are favourites with fare-paying customers.

I may have mentioned it before, but the best place in the world to photograph wild Mute Swans is at the Abbotsbury Swannery in Dorset. Mum and baby getting close together.

A dangerous place to be if you're in the flight path of a landing swan!

This baby British Otter cub had just taken his first swim in a bath, and loved to wrap himself in a bath towel.

Asian Short-clawed Otter cubs from
Dartmoor Wildlife Park in Devon,
with eyes bigger than their bellies.

A spectacular Harris Hawk
at Saker Falconry.

This otter cub looks frightened to death as he cuddles his owner whilst sucking his fingers.

Easy does it... Everybody's favourite insect, the ladybird,
wandering around a back-lit flower.

The horrendous story of the cat who was caught in a gin trap in Topsham, Devon, and had to chew off his own leg to escape. He was still loyal to his owner, nuzzling up to his leg, even though he was still recovering from an operation.

Mr Woo the albino wallaby keeps dry as the raindrops
keep falling on his head at Secret World Wildlife Rescue, whilst a
glimpse of a pure white albino pheasant in a field near Thorverton
was a sight for sore eyes.

Three goslings taking a foot rest.

If you're a duck and a pair of swans are landing right behind you... get out of the way quick.

A young cygnet hitching a ride and keeping warm under mum's feathers.

Share and share alike, exactly what this pair of dogs did on the beach at Lyme Regis
with the family frisby, whilst the terrier shuts his eyes as he makes a save.

When the story broke that new agricultural rules meant that farm animals had to have toys to play with to keep themselves amused, I wondered how the young pigs would react at Kennford Farm Shop near Exeter. As it happens, they were very interested and soon punctured the rubber ring.

Katrina takes her pet goose for flying lessons near Whimple, Devon.

As we were all going through a hot spell, Duffy the goose was kept cool via a watering can. He didn't seem to mind, after all it was simply water off a duck's back!

Summer visitors to Britain don't fly any faster than Swifts. Almost as soon as they
get here they are looking for nesting sights and can squeeze into the smallest of places.

In a news story relating to hunting on the brink of being banned, I was sent to the kennels and couldn't resist this picture of the hound pups just being inquisitive.

This seal pup had hauled himself out of the water and on to the Cobb at Lyme Regis in Dorset for several days in a row. I felt I'd got to know him until I tried to stroke his back, and he showed me a perfect set of teeth!

Marauding seagulls are not everyone's cup of tea, but I love them, especially when there's food to be stolen, scoffed and fought over.

Coot chicks are not the prettiest of babies I have ever seen, but they were entertaining as they pestered their mother for food by battering on her beak.

A visiting circus took their small herd of young African Elephants into the River Exe at Tiverton in Devon for a wash and a splash. At the time I couldn't help wondering if ever before in the long history of the river elephants bathed in it's waters.

All mouths open in these two pictures...
The guillemot had his beak cleaned
following an oil spill in the
English Channel, while the three blue-tit
babies are eagerly waiting for a
meal to arrive.

During the Queen's Golden Jubilee even the animals got close up and personal
with the Union Flag, including this Weimaraner and donkey foal.

New arrivals at Paignton Zoo in Devon often make the headlines. This delightful baby chameleon had sticky feet and could grip anything, while the pencil demonstrated just how small the creature was.

This tiny Harvest Mouse is invited to return to the wild by staff at Secret World Wildlife Rescue in Somerset.

A baby Grey Squirrel takes his milk from a syringe, sitting in a hand of human kindness.

This tame fox enjoys a nice cup of tea in the morning at the Dartmoor Wildlife Park in Devon.

The eyes have it... Three baby Dormice pose on an oak tree twig at Secret World Wildlife Rescue.

Jaguar and tiger cubs at Dartmoor Wildlife Park in Devon.

A hedgehog makes his way through fallen autumn leaves.

Sunshine and dark curtains were effective lighting when photographing these baby Dormice, aptly named the 'Munch Bunch' when they appeared in the newspapers.

A police dog new recruit tries on his uniform before being put
through his paces at Devon & Cornwall Police HQ in Exeter.

Farmer Chris Burnett really did stir up a hornets' nest when his farm machinery accidentally broke one up on his Somerset farm. Although the nest was doomed the dedicated hornets kept bringing food back to their offspring.

I couldn't tell who was the more excited in meeting each other, the little girl or the young hedgehog!

Foxy, the tame fox, loves to play on the lawn at Dartmoor Wildlife Park near Plymouth.

Ellie West has a bit of fun with her pet Eagle Owl called Eddie. Well that's what he had been called since he was a chick, until a vet broke the news that Eddie was in fact Edwina. Yes, Eddie is a girl!

Edwina the Eagle Owl makes a stark contrast against a dramatic sky.

A reconstruction of how a hedgehog
nearly choked to death on discarded
rubbish, and *(above)* an African Pygmy
Hedgehog with large ears seen in
Newton Abbot.

Labrador pups, as cute as you like.

I waited quite along time for these two cock pheasants to start fighting, and it was all over in a flash.
I am still not sure if the two birds actually made contact or if it was all a bluff.

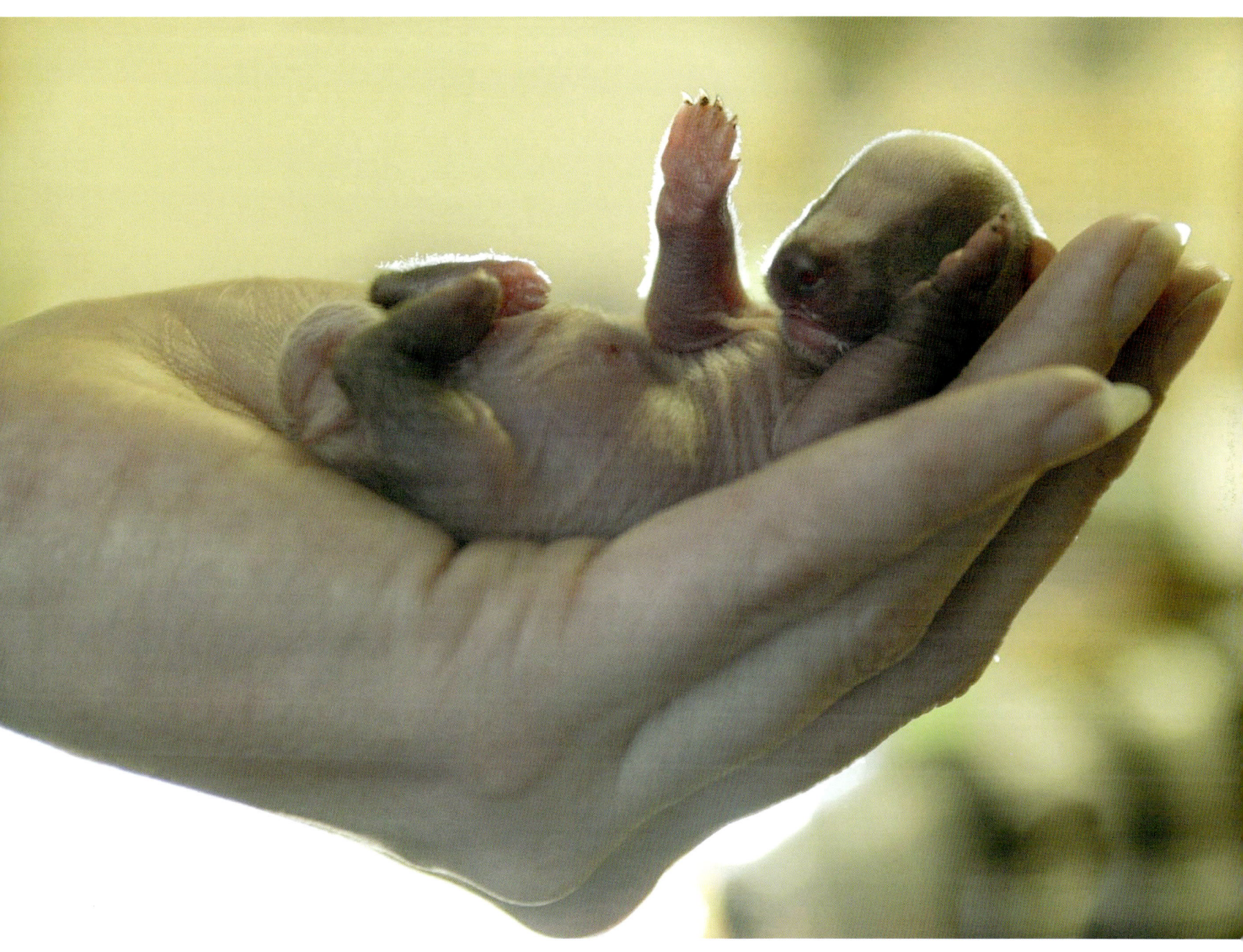

The youngest badger cub I have ever photographed. The cub was abandoned by its mother just hours after it was born, and for me it represents the vast knowledge and experience that the team at Secret World Wildlife Rescue has in bringing up the cub by hand.

Badger cub making a mug of himself.

This cub's first encounter with a string of sausages ended up with this badger giving them a cuddle.

What a diver... A massive splash for small dog as he takes the plunge into a pond.

Being born in the winter for this young donkey foal meant he had to wear a special coat that was designed for a dog, whilst *(above)* a pair of unwanted youngsters at the RSPCA were getting to know each other for the first time.

This was the occasion when several lost tortoises had been handed in to Secret World Wildlife Rescue with more than a few people claiming them. So a tortoise identification parade was arranged so the people could make a positive ID.

A magnificent Exmoor Red Deer stag keeping an eye on his ladies and watching out for other stags who may want to challenge him to a duel.

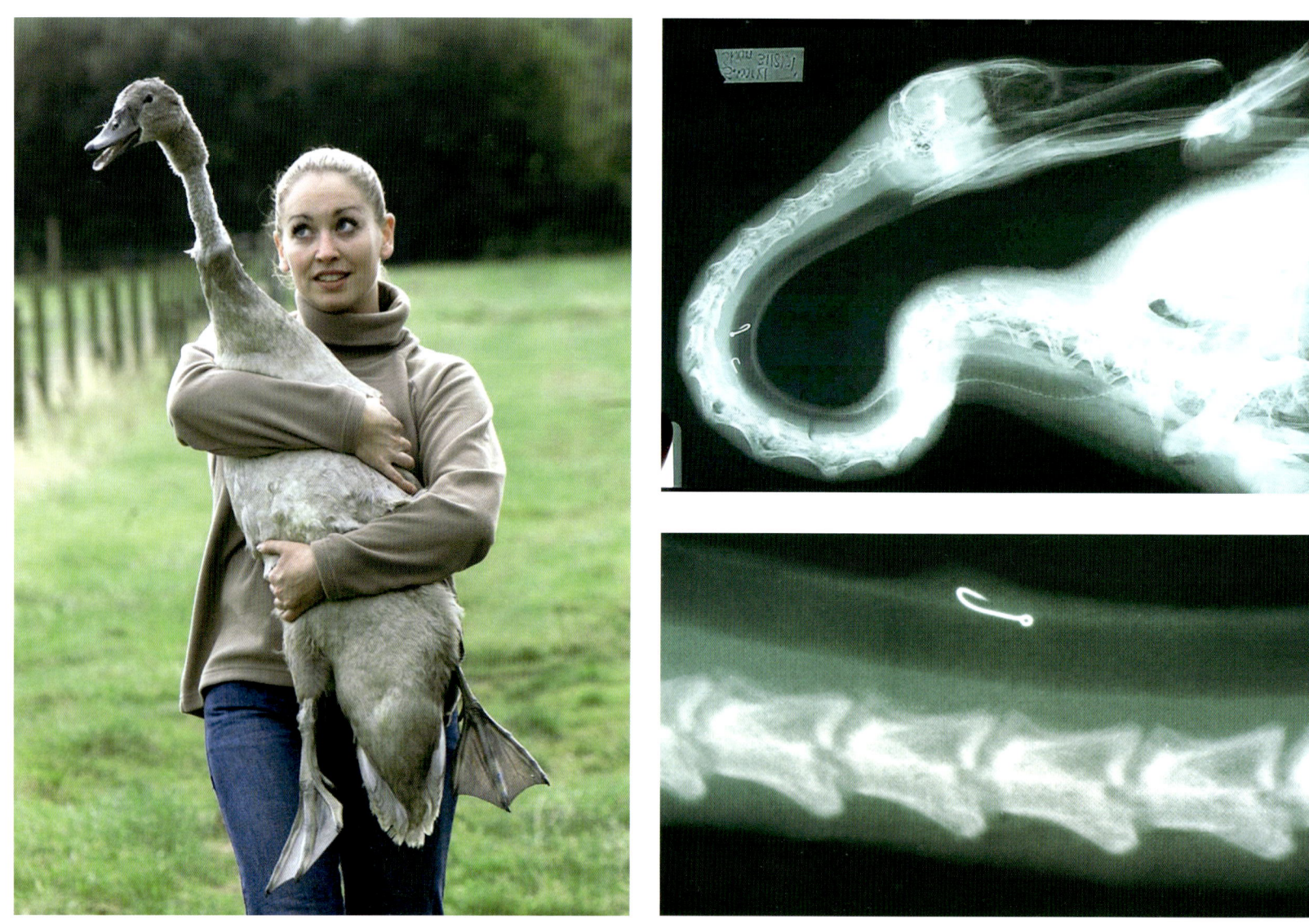

Nikki Hawkins takes a young swan back to his pool as he recuperates from an operation to recover fishing tackle he had swallowed. The X-rays show the fish hook stuck fast inside the bird's neck.

Swimming home at the end of the day on the River Axe in East Devon.

Sharing a stick on the beach.

Hatched in December, this little duckling needed
all the help he could get in keeping out the winter chill.

Just finishing off his dinner, this otter saved the tail until last.

It was the expression on this tame fox's face that did it for me as he prowled around the lawn at the Dartmoor Wildlife Park near Plymouth.

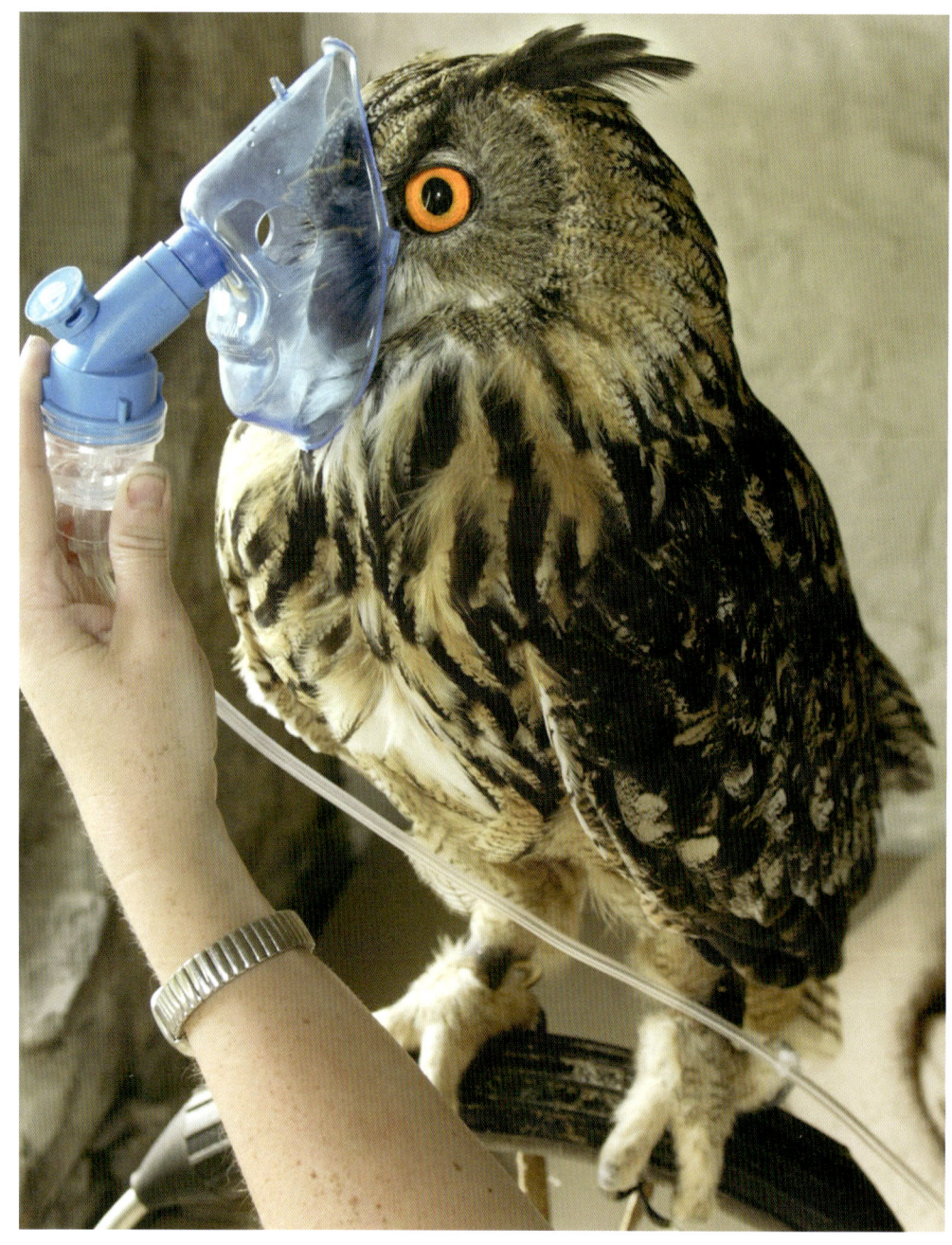

This Eagle Owl, suffering from a form of asthma,
being treated with a nebuliser twice a day.

The Eagle Owl off his perch and ready to work with his falconer.

A tiny orphaned Roe Deer amongst the wildflowers in Somerset.

Baby Roe Deer out for a walk for
the first time at Secret World Wildlife Rescue.

A pasty face with pink eyes, yes, it's an albino
hedgehog being brought up by human kindness.

Great Dane Shannon with terrier
Megan, the best of friends who
play together all day.

More fun and games from
this irrepressible pair.

Seagulls fighting over a mackerel at Lyme Regis.

Chips with everything is exactly what the gulls like on the South Coast,
and when they are hungry they are not too fussy where they get them from.

Warm, dry and highly visible, four winter lambs in raincoats make a colourful sight at Wylde Meadow Farm in Dorset.

Almost as though they were saying good morning to each other at Dartmoor Wildlife Park.

An elegant swan's neck makes an interesting contrast against thick weed on the Grand Western Canal near Tiverton.

This Mandarin Duck looks almost too perfect to have been created by Mother Nature,
What a perfect little bird, with every feather in place.

A comical pair who share the limelight. Both the African Grey Parrot, called Jasper, and Murphy the Dachshund, never stop arguing. While the dog grumbles and growls in dog-speak, the parrot talks in English and tells the dog to 'Get out'.

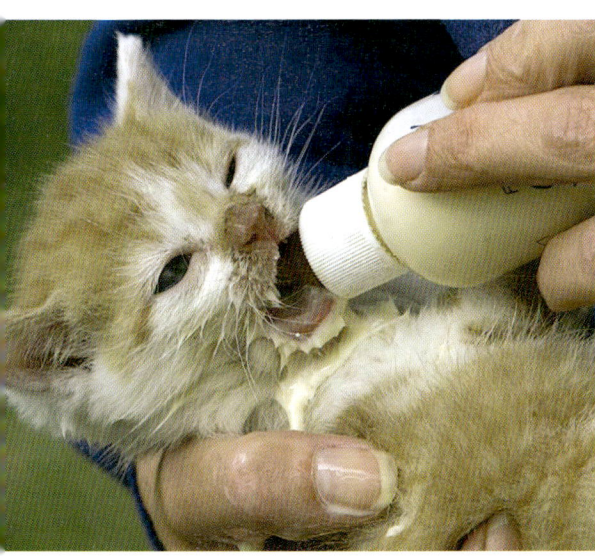

Unwanted kittens up for grabs, and the tender moment of a tiny kitten being hand-fed to keep him alive.

Tree climbing comes naturally to big cats, especially this Jaguar at the Dartmoor Wildlife Park.

Pegged out and waiting for new owners, Spaniel pups hang loose.

Duffy the tame goose drifts through the crowds at the Devon County Show.

It's a dog's life for this young Yorkshire Terrier pup at his first photocall with a pair of Indian Runner ducks

Their last photocall before being prepared for release; four small badger cubs hand-reared at Secret World Wildlife Rescue.

Trying to photograph a swallow in flight is almost an impossible task. I found that the best way
to do it was to focus on a narrow patch of water and wait for the swallow to come to you.

A newspaper picture for Easter at Pennywell Farm in Buckfastleigh. The three ducklings were perfectly happy to pose with an ostrich egg, and I love the stance and expression of the one on the right.

Easter ducklings.

Indian Runner ducks in a huddle at Bodmin in Cornwall.

All born at the same time, the kitten and ducklings getting on famously in Cornwall.

They probably wouldn't be so friendly in the wild, but these two cubs accepted each other without squabbles.

Daylight robbery as Mute Swans at the Abbotsbury Swannery help
themselves to the grain from the swanherd's wheelbarrow.

Springtime, and a fox cub peeks out from under the daffodils.

A remarkable story of the Devon goose who talked on a mobile phone to his owner who was on a station platform in Scotland.

An early-morning swan rises
off the lagoon at the Abbotsbury
Swannery, his massive wings on
the downbeat as he gains height.

Almost weightless, a Harvest
Mouse on a daffodil.

The size of this little pig could only be illustrated by the fact that the crocuses were taller than he was at Woodlands.

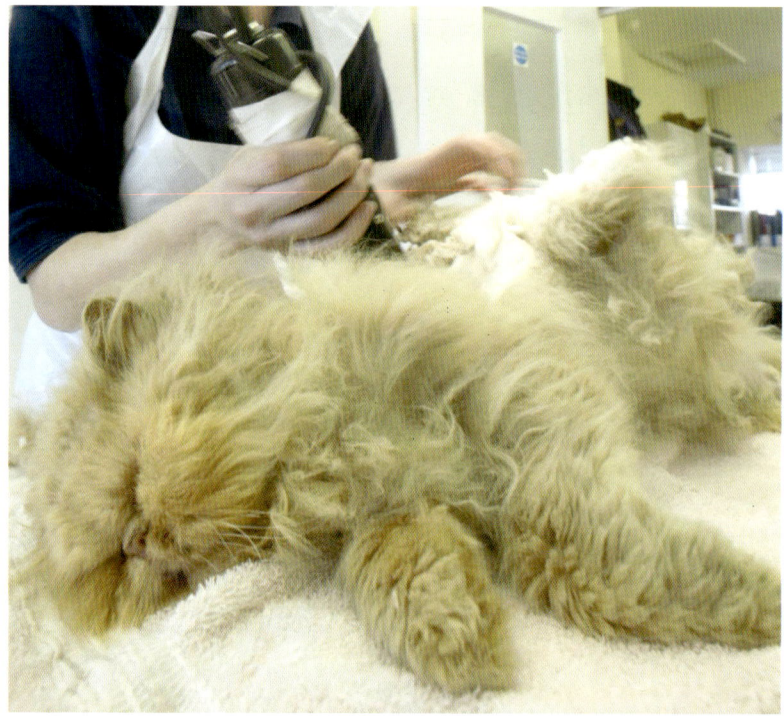

I had seen it before, but only twice; when Persian cats are not brushed regularly their fur becomes matted and that means a trip to the vet, a general anaesthetic and a total body shave except the feet and head.

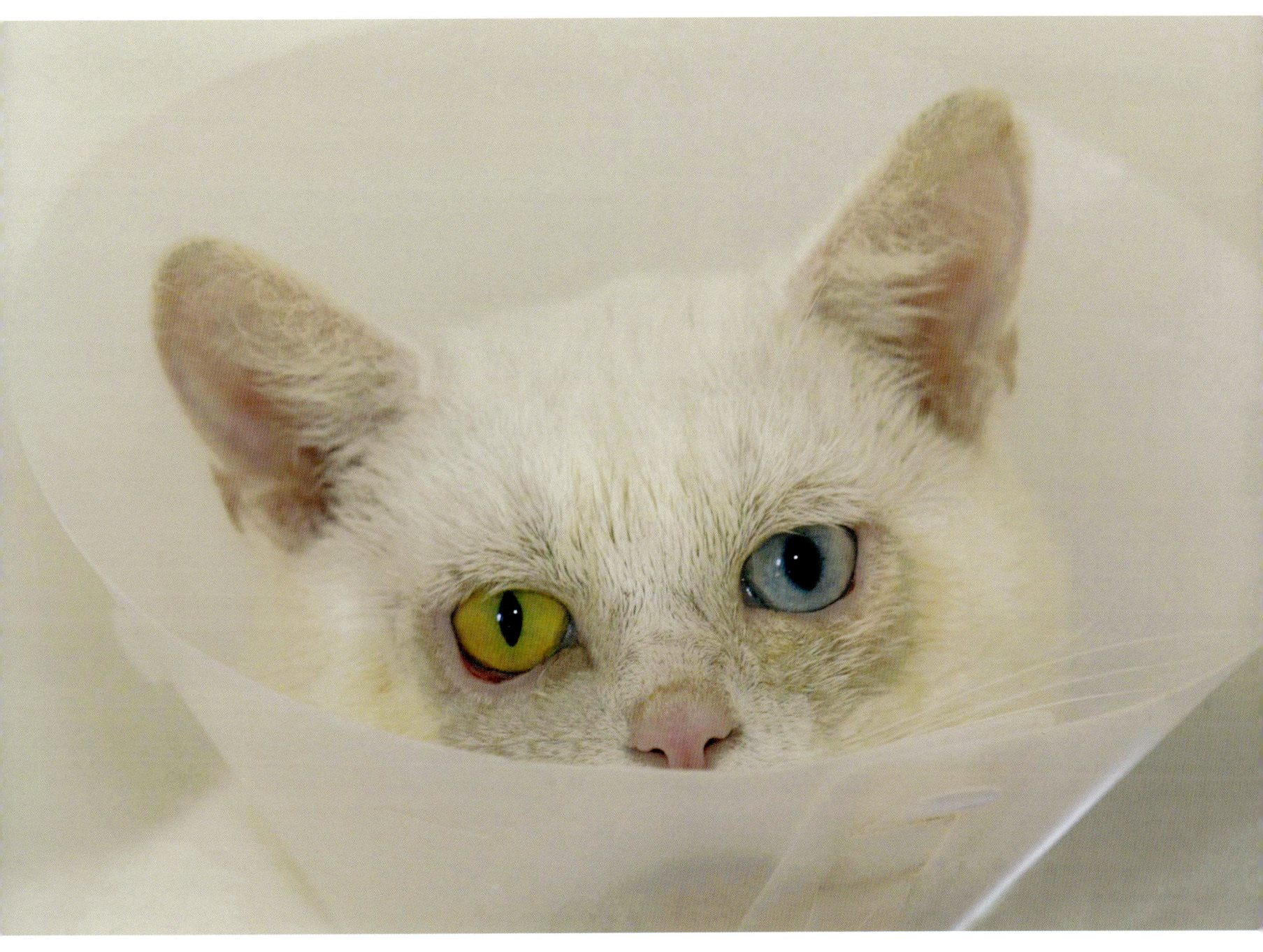

The colour of his eyes were unusual enough but the white hood around his neck looked almost surreal.
This cat was recovering from an operation for entropia, when the eyelashes grow inwards.

I was at Secret World Wildlife Rescue looking for a cute springtime picture involving daffodils, and the first picture in the can was the Harvest Mouse on the bright yellow flower. Then I saw the staff checking on three baby Dormice who were beginning to wake from their winter hibernation. This vision of the mice still asleep on the flowers entered my mind and the whole shoot was completed in a minute, with the mice none the wiser.

The hibernating Dormouse having a small stretch as he begins to wake up for the summer.

Nearly ready for release, a Little Owl waiting for his feathers to grow and then back to the wild.

A Guinea Fowl chick being hand-reared but a long way off flying yet.

In the blue corner a lone moorhen, and in the red corner three marauding coots. The problem on the Grand Western Canal, at Sampford Peverell, was that the coots wanted the same nesting site as the moorhen, and the moorhen was there first. All hell broke loose for about a minute, and although the moorhen was outnumbered she came out the winner and the three coots scuttled off down the canal.

On a freezing cold day these two foxes were curled up asleep on a bank on Exminster Marshes, which speaks volumes for the effectiveness of their winter coats. Whilst *(above)* a pair of cubs enjoy their meal at the RSPCA.

Hydrotherapy for dogs to get those arthritic joints moving again. The
Yorkshire Terrier wore a lifejacket as he completed a few lengths in the pool.

Spike, who died last year, was officially the oldest cat in the world and had a *Guinness Book of Records* certificate to prove it. He was quite agile for a cat born in the 1970s, but was a nightmare to photograph because he didn't like cameras very much. Nevertheless he was a handsome old chap and gave his owners a great deal of pleasure during his long life.

When you're hatched out of season, and the weather turns chilly, a custom-made sock comes in handy to keep this gosling warm.

The last thing you need when indulging in a spot of sunbathing is a cheeky seagull to start cleaning out your ears, and then your feet.

This little Bison calf at Paignton Zoo put up with the gull for quite a while before getting up and quietly walking off.

Any sighting of a Kingfisher is a noteworthy occasion, but to get
this close to the bird whilst he was fishing was a bit special.

The BBC's Mr Blobby swaps places with the sealion.

Two newborns meet each other for the first time. The baby rabbit settled
for a quick sniff whilst the tiny robin totally ignored his new friend.

A rare sight, the Dartford Warbler; a spectacular little bird with stunning red eyes.

Siberian Tigers are the largest cats in the world; this one had just eaten and flopped down in the grass for a lazy afternoon.

A bad hair day for the Afghan Hound as he races around a track in Somerset.

The picture that's been done a thousand times before – but I couldn't resist the spectacular display by this peacock.

Peacock feathers mask the duckling as he sits on the fence.

This crafty fox cub knew I was waiting for him to collect the rabbit I had just seen his mother leave for him.
He spent a few minutes staring me out through the hedge, then quickly nipped out to grab his dinner.

A piece of turnip as a treat for the little wallaby who was orphaned and growing up in an old haversack instead of his mother's pouch.